SCIENTIFIC AMERICAN

EVERYTHING YOU NEED FOR

SIMPLE SCIENCE FAIR PROJECTS

Grades 3-5

by Bob Friedhoffer

Illustrated by Ernie Colon

CHELSEA CLUBHOUSE

An Imprint of Chelsea House Publishers

This book is dedicated

To BRIAN SCHWARTZ—

A mentor,

A friend,

A mensch.

Scientific American: Everything You Need for Simple Science Fair Projects

Copyright © 2006 by Byron Preiss Visual Publications, Inc.
In cooperation with Scientific American and Chelsea House Publishers
Published in the United States of America in 2006 by Chelsea House Publishers.

Chelsea Clubhouse
An imprint of Chelsea House Publishers
132 West 31st Street
New York NY 10001

For Library of Congress Cataloging-in-Publication
data is available from the publisher.
ISBN 0-7910-9054-X

Chelsea House books are available at special discounts when purchased in bulk quantities for businesses, associations, institutions, or sales promotions. Please call our Special Sales Department in New York at (212) 967-8800 or (800) 322-8755.

You can find Chelsea House on the World Wide Web at
http://www.chelseahouse.com

Edited by Howard Zimmerman
Associate Editor: Charles Curtis
Cover design by Andy Davies
Interior design by Gilda Hannah
Interior illustrations by Ernie Colon

Printed in the United States of America

Bang PKG 10 9 8 7 6 5 4 3 2 1

This book is printed on acid-free paper.

CONTENTS

BOB FRIEDHOFFER teaches teachers how to teach science in the classroom. He is also a touring, practicing stage magician, and many of his illusions represent basic science principles. Friedhoffer is a member of the National Science Teachers Association, the American Association of Physics Teachers, the New York Academy of Science, the Academy of Magical Arts, the American Federation of TV and Radio Artists, and the Screen Actors Guild, among others.

Friedhoffer's books on science and magic include: *Yet More Magic Tricks, Science Facts* (2001); *Old Magic with Today's Science* (2001); *Physics Lab in the Sporting Goods Store* (2001); *Physics Lab in the Playground* (2001); *Physics Lab in the Supermarket* (1999); *Physics Lab in the Home* (1997); *Magic and Perception* (1996); *Toying Around with Science* (1995); "The Scientific Magic Series" (1992, six titles): *Matter and Energy, Forces, Motion and Energy, Heat, Sound, Electricity and Magnetism,* and *Light; Magic Tricks, Science Facts* (1990); *How to Haunt a House for Halloween* (1988).

RESOURCES FOR SCIENCE FAIR EXPERIMENTS

Supplies. All of the materials required for the experiments in this book can be found at home or in "houseware supplies" stores and "hardware" stores.

Information and further ideas. It is recommended that readers visit one or more of the following World Wide Web sites for more information on the science involved in this book's experiments, as well as for ideas for other experiments in the same areas of science. If you do not have a computer with an Internet hookup at home, try your school or local library.

http://www.ipl.org/div/kidspace/projectguide/
http://www.sciserv.org/isef/
http://energyquest.ca.gov/projects/index.html
http://www.ars.usda.gov/is/kids/fair/ideasframe.htm
http://kids.gov/k_science.htm
http://canadaonline.about.com/cs/sciencefairideas/
http://www.physics.uwo.ca/sfair/sflinks.htm
http://www.cdli.ca/sciencefairs/
http://www.scifair.org
http://homeworkspot.com/sciencefair/
http://school.discovery.com/sciencefaircentral/scifairstudio/ideas.html
http://www.all-science-fair-projects.com/category0.html

HAVE FUN WITH YOUR SCIENCE FAIR PROJECT

*B*y entering a science fair, you investigate a small part of the natural world around you and find out how it works, or does not work. You can discover things by yourself rather than read it out of a book or have someone tell you. *Your* science fair project should be an investigation that interests *you*. This book provides over two dozen experiments, but do not feel that these are the only possible selections. They have been supplied as examples of possible science fair projects. You may use one of these or, if you wish, you may use these as models for your own experiment and display.

One important thing to keep in mind is that experiments can be successful, whether they prove your point or not. In either case, you will have learned something about that area of science. In all cases, these science-fair experiments should be done *with the help of an adult*. It cannot be stated too often: ADULT SUPERVISION FOR ALL EXPERIMENTS is strongly recommended. Some experiments involve using knives and other sharp objects. Some require the use of water or a heat source. Some require the use of electrical equipment. And, therefore, it is once again strongly recommended that you have ADULT SUPERVISION FOR ALL EXPERIMENTS. It may be a family member, a friend, a teacher, or someone else from school.

Because there are so many different kinds of science, you should look for a topic that will not only teach you about the world around you, but will also make the project personal and fun. Before you attempt to put together an experiment, do some research on your subject at a library or on the Internet. Talk to your teacher about what you're inter-

ested in. After doing this preliminary work, you should be able to come up with a "hypothesis"—an assumption that can be tested for accuracy—and an experimental method to confirm or disprove it. Your hypothesis should be in the form of a statement (*Capillary action helps water rise inside of plants*).

When one undertakes a science fair project, the method described below should be used as a guide for your work:

1. Describe the problem/question. What do you want to investigate?
2. Develop a hypothesis. What do you think the experiment will prove?
3. Perform the experimental procedures and collect data.
4. Arrange and assess the collected data. Compare the actual results of your experiment to your hypothesis.
6. Think about your experimental results and make your conclusions. Was your hypothesis correct?
7. Communicate the results to others.

Safety and Permission

You should always decide upon and perform your experiments with safety in mind. Take all safety precautions that are recommended, and others that may not be listed.

If the project involves items that can get into your eyes, wear safety goggles. If electricity is going to be used, make sure that you can not get a shock from the equipment. Do not put experimental items into your mouth—unless it is fresh food and part of the experiment. Always get an adult's permission to undertake all of the steps in the project. If you are going to use paint, or nails or tape, etc. make sure that it is OK with your parents *before* you start. And, as noted above, it is necessary to HAVE ADULT SUPERVISION FOR ALL EXPERIMENTS.

Data Entry

It is important that you keep a "lab notebook." This should be a notebook, of any size you wish, that ONLY has information about your experiment in it, from your hypothesis to the results of the performed experiment. You should collect all of the information from you experiments in an organized manner, which will help you to present it later. If your experiment takes more than a single day, you should have a separate entry for each day of the experiment. If your experimental results can be described in numbers (inches, ounces, pounds, length of time, number of times tried, etc.) it would be helpful for your display to include this information.

Presentation

When your experiment has been completed, you will want to be able to present it so that your classmates and teachers can see what you have done. In many cases, you will be entering your experiment into a school science fair. How will you present your experiment? How will you show your work and the results? There should be two parts to the presentation of your science experiment.

Tabletop Display of the Experiment

You will need to show the stages of your experiment. This is usually done on a tabletop, but it doesn't have to be. Some experiments are too large to fit on top of a table, and some just need more space. But you will want to display all parts of the experiment that you can. You must show the results of your experiment—how it worked out. The illustrations in this book show how each experiment would look if done according to the "experimental procedure."

You may also wish to place on your tabletop display your lab notebook with the records of your experiment.

Data Display (charts, graphs, etc.)

There are many ways to arrange your data in order to present it with your final display. You can use a chart, in which you use rows and columns to compare two different observations (variables) against each other. Most of the data you collect can be organized into a table.

You can use a graph to display your data. There are many types of graphs, but three that you may find useful are bar graphs, line graphs and pie charts. A bar graph uses different sized bars to indicate the data you've collected. If one bar is higher than another, it means a larger size was recorded.

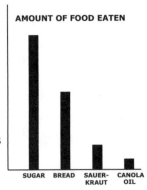

A line graph shows how your experiment was affected by variables. You can chart different points through-

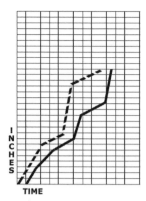

out the graph with each point representing a piece of data. By connecting the dots, your can see how your data changed as the two variables had an effect in the experiment.

A pie chart is used when measuring percentages: it splits your data into different sections like slices of a pie. The bigger the slice of the chart, the larger the percentage of your total data.

Not only should you write down all of the numerical information you get from your experiments, but you should also place all of your thoughts and observations about the project in the notebook, such as:

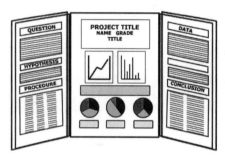

WHAT ANTS EAT AND WHY

CANOLA OIL

BREAD

SUGAR

SAUERKRAUT

What area do I want to discover something about or examine?

What is the exact question about that area?

Did I get my parent's permission?

What do I think the conclusion of the experiment will show?

Make a list of the necessary materials for the project.

How you arranged everything to perform the experiment.

What were the results of the experiment? How much, how far, how hot, how cold, etc.

Was my hypothesis proven or disproven? (Either one is good.)

A Report for the Tabletop Display

Usually in a science fair experiment, you present your information as a report in sentence and paragraph form explaining every-

thing you have written in your lab book. Start by presenting your hypothesis and explaining your step-by-step procedure of how you did the experiment. You should then display your data, followed by a section that explains what the data indicates about your experiment. Finally and most important, there should be a few paragraphs about your conclusions as you discuss whether your hypothesis was confirmed or disproven. When you finish your report, try to find a way to explain the experimental data and results on display panels. You would like the information to be easily read and understood by anyone examining the display. Displays are frequently presented as three-panel charts with the information applied as follows.

The upper portion of the left side panel usually supplies the problem/question under study and your hypothesis. The lower portion of the left side panel usually gives an overview of the experimental procedure.

PROJECT TITLE
NAME GRADE
TITLE

QUESTION

HYPOTHESIS

PROCEDURE

DATA

CONCLUSION

The upper portion of the center panel usually has your name, the name of the project, your teacher's name, your grade, and your school name. The lower portion of the center panel is often used for charts, photographs, and illustrations. The right hand panel generally shows a summary of the data with the results you have observed and your conclusion. The tabletop in front of the three panels is frequently used to display the experiment itself. Try to make the experiment on display available to all who walk by so you can demonstrate what you have done. And have fun!

IDENTIFYING SOLIDS, LIQUIDS, AND GASES

Explanation

There are three types, or states, of matter. They are: solids, liquids and gasses.

A solid has an exact shape and exact volume. (Volume is the amount of space that a substance takes up.) Solids include: trees, school books, pens and pencils, running shoes, the bottles drinks come in, bricks, and dirt.

A liquid is a substance that has no definite shape but has a definite volume. Liquids include: water, paint, ink, chocolate syrup and gasoline.

A gas is a substance that has no definite shape and no definite volume. Examples of gases are: the air we breathe, the bubbles you see in a bottle of soda, the fuel that is used for gas-fired barbecue grills, and that nasty-smelling stuff when you pass gas.

Experimental Question

How can we identify whether a substance is a solid, a liquid, or a gas without actually seeing the substance?

BACKGROUND INFORMATION

Molecules are the smallest parts of any substance.

In solids, the molecules are usually close together and rarely move about. This allows a solid to keep its shape.

Molecules of liquids are usually close together, but they can move around easily. This means that a liquid does not have an exact shape, but will take the shape of any container large enough to enclose the liquid's volume.

Gas molecules move around quickly and are far apart. A gas can be compressed into a smaller space or may expand into a larger space.

Necessary Materials

- Beach sand
- A pint of latex paint: black, blue, or red
- A small paint brush
- 3 empty, clean, plastic water bottles with screw-on caps (the bottles should all be the same size)
- A small, plastic cereal bowl
- A plastic catch basin
- A plastic teaspoon
- A magnifying glass
- A large zipper-type plastic storage bag
- A soda straw

Preparation

1. Remove the labels from the bottles.
2. Paint the outside surface of each bottle, holding it by sticking a finger or two into the top. Make sure that the paint is thick enough so that you cannot see what is in any of the bottles.
3. Wait for the paint to dry.
4. Totally fill one bottle with sand. After you have some sand in the bottle, pick up the bottle and gently tap the bottom on the tabletop. This allows the sand to fill little spaces that are sometimes between the grains. Do this tapping a few times as you fill the bottle. Leave no air at the top.
5. Screw the cap tightly onto the bottle.
6. Completely fill another bottle with water. When you screw the cap onto the bottle make sure that there is no air in the bottle. You can do this by filling a large tub with water, placing the bottle into the tub so that the mouth of the bottle is completely underwater, and then screwing the cap on the bottle.
7. Leave the third bottle empty. Screw the cap tightly onto the bottle. (**SEE ILLUSTRATION "A."**)

A

Procedure

1. Squeeze the first bottle firmly (but not hard enough to pop the top off). Note your observations.
2. Squeeze the second bottle the same way. Again, note your observations.
3. Squeeze the third bottle the same way. Take notes. (**SEE ILLUSTRATION "B."**)

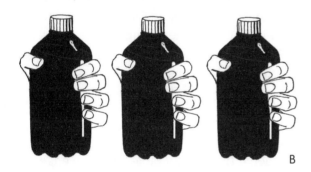

B

Results

One bottle will maintain its shape during and after squeezing. It must be filled with a solid substance. One bottle will change shape while you squeeze it, but will go back to its original shape when you let go. That bottle must be filled with a liquid. The bottle filled with air will change shape and remain in the shape in which you squeezed it. (**SEE ILLUSTRATION "C."**)

Conclusions

The bottles actually act like the molecules of the substances inside them. The sand (solid) hardly moves. The water molecules (liquid)

stay together but move a little bit more than the solid. And the air molecules move so much that its easy to change the shape of the container they're in. By squeezing the bottles and observing them during and after squeezing, we can identify which one holds a solid, which holds a liquid, and which holds a gas.

C

SECONDARY EXPERIMENT

Experimental Question

How can we show that solids in containers maintain their shapes while liquids take the shape of their container?

Procedure

1. Taking some extra sand, pour it into the bowl. Not a single grain changes shape.
2. Fill another bowl with water. It does change its shape to the contours of the bowl.
3. Look at a grain of sand on your hand with a magnifying glass and remember its shape.
4. Place the grain of sand in a teaspoon. Look at it with the magnifying glass and see that it maintains its shape.
5. Do the same with a drop of water and the teaspoon. Remember its shape both on your hand and in the spoon and observe that, once again, the shape of water changes when placed on differently shaped surfaces.

HOW TO BUILD AND OPERATE A SIPHON

Explanation: A siphon is a device that allows a liquid to drain from a container at an elevated height to a lower area without tilting or putting a hole in the bottom of the container. Many people believe that the water is pushed through the tube (siphon) by air pressure.

BACKGROUND INFORMATION

The cohesive force is easy to see on your kitchen counter. Water forms puddles on a flat table surface because the molecules that make up water are attracted to each other. If there were no cohesive force, the water would not form puddles or drops. It would spread and become a layer of water, only one molecule deep, practically impossible to see.

As water fills a siphon's entire length, cohesion, along with gravity, act as forces on the liquid. The molecules of water at the lowest end of the siphon are pulled down by gravity until they leave the siphon. Each molecule of water carries neighboring molecules of water along with it in a continuous column that flows into the catch basin.

Imagine that you have a fish tank filled with a gallon of water, stones and plants. It needs to be cleaned out. You can't just pour the water into the sink since it is too heavy to lift, and everything else would go down the drain with the water. Instead, you place a tube in the tank and hold it so that it drains into a basin that is lower than the tank itself. After sucking in a little air through the outflow end of the tube, the water seems to drain by itself without the aid of something pumping it out of the tank.

That is not so. The force that pulls a liquid through a siphon is its own cohesive force combined with gravity. The cohesive force is the attraction that water molecules have for each other. (The "cohesive force" is the attraction that molecules have for neighboring molecules, allowing them to clump, or stick together.)

Experimental Question: How can we get water to flow from one container to another?

Necessary Materials

NOTE: Only do this experiment over a sink, bathtub, or other catch basin.

- A 3-foot length of $1\frac{1}{4}''$ (inside diameter) clear, flexible, plastic tubing, and a 6-foot length of the same tubing
- A plastic fish bowl or fish tank
- A heavy, clear glass or clear plastic pitcher

Preparation

1. Fill the pitcher with clean, lukewarm water.
2. Place it on top of a table, near the edge.
3. Place the empty fish bowl (or fish tank) below the pitcher, either on the floor or on the seat of a level chair or stool. (It must be close enough to the pitcher so that the tubing will reach from one container to the other.)
4. Place one end of the plastic tubing into the pitcher so that it just touches the bottom. This will be called the "inner end."
5. Allow the other end to hang outside of the pitcher. This will be called the "outflow end."

Procedure Part One

1. Take the outflow end of the tube between your lips and draw upon it until the water arrives in your mouth.

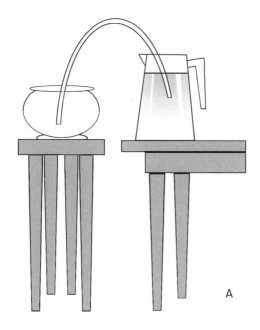

A

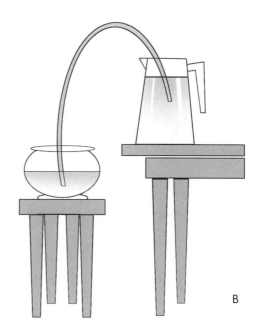

B

2. Squeeze the tip of the tube tightly with your fingertips, so that the water will not run back into the pitcher.

3. Hold the outflow end higher than the inner end. Point it down. Stop squeezing the out-flow end of the tube. What happens? (The water in the outflow side will not run into the fish bowl.) (**SEE ILLUSTRATION "A."**)

5. Take the outflow end of the tube between your lips and draw upon it until the water arrives in your mouth.

6. Squeeze the tip of the tube tightly with your fingertips, so that the water will not run back into the pitcher.

7. Place the outflow end into the fish bowl, which is on a chair or stool that is lower than the table top.

8. Stop squeezing the end of the tube. What happens? The water in the tube should start running into the fish bowl. (**SEE**

ILLUSTRATION "B.") It should continue to run until the water level in the pitcher lowers to the opening of the tube's inflow side.

Results: Water will flow from the tube and will continue to do so until the water in the pitcher drains to the same level as the opening of the inner end.

Conclusions: We can use a siphon to make water flow from one container to another. The attraction that water molecules have for each other (or, cohesion) is the reason that the water flows into the siphon. By sucking on the tube, you bring the flow of water from the inner end to the outflow end. As long as the outflow end is lower than the inner end, cohesion and gravity will cause the water to flow. (See the next page for a secondary experiment with your siphon.)

SECONDARY EXPERIMENT

Experimental Question
How will factors like height, length and placement of the tube effect a siphon?

Necessary Materials
Use the same table-top setup as the main experiment.

Preparation
None necessary.

Procedure
1. Fill the container with water and start the siphon flowing. As the water flows, raise the outflow opening until it is level with the inflow opening. What happens?

   When the height of the outflow is equal to that of the inflow, the water should stop running through the siphon.
2. Use a very long (5–6 feet) plastic tube. Put most of the tube into the pitcher.

   Q. What do you think will happen when you try to start the siphon?

   A. As long as the outflow end is lower than the inner end, the siphon will still work, no matter the length of the tube in the container.
3. Place enough of the long tube into the container so that it touches the bottom. Start the siphon as you did before.

   Q. What happens if you coil the outflow end, always keeping the opening below that of the inner end?

   A. The water keeps on flowing.

   Q. What if you were to raise the middle of the outflow tube higher than the inner end opening, all the while keeping the outflow end beneath the inflow?

   A. The water will keep on flowing.

Results
When the height of the outflow is equal to that of the inner end, the water stops running through the siphon. When the outflow end of the siphon is higher than the inner end, water will not run through the siphon.

Conclusion
As long as the outflow end of a siphon is lower than the inner end, water will flow from one container to another regardless of the siphon's length or placement.

REMOVING HEAT FROM AN OBJECT

Explanation

We can remove heat from things (make them cooler) through the process of evaporation. Evaporation occurs when a liquid becomes a gas. This is the method through which water turns into *water vapor*, which is a gas. When water molecules on the surface of a liquid turn to water vapor, they generally rise and take with them some of the heat from the surface they have just left.

Experimental Question

How can we cool a liquid by applying heat?

Necessary Materials

- A full jar of rubbing alcohol
- A metal meat thermometer
- A paper cup
- Sticky tape
- A hair dryer
- Scissors

Preparation

1. Cut the paper cup down so that it is 3″ high.
2. Tape the cup down to your working surface.

BACKGROUND INFORMATION

Different factors increase evaporation. One is moving air. A breeze will increase evaporation by carrying away water vapor molecules before they can settle back onto the liquid. Heat will increase evaporation by making the water molecules move faster, which gives more molecules a chance to move away from the liquid.

Procedure

1. Open the bottle of rubbing alcohol and measure its temperature with the thermometer. Record the temperature.
2. Pour enough alcohol into the cup so that it is filled half way.
3. Place the thermometer into the cup and measure the temperature of the alcohol. Record the temperature.
4. Hold the hair dryer 12″ away from the cup, turn it on **"Low"** and aim the airflow at an angle so that it only grazes the top of the cup. (**SEE ILLUSTRATION.**) Record the temperature as you use the hair dryer.

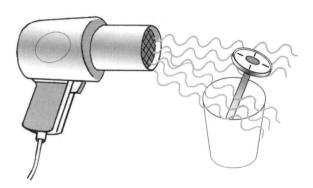

Results

The temperature of the alcohol in the cup should start to fall. As the top layer of alcohol starts to evaporate, heat is taken from the remaining liquid.

Conclusions

Evaporation decreases the temperature of liquids as they are converted into gas. The application of moving air and heat are two ways in which evaporation may be increased. Using a hair dryer—a heat source—we can cause a liquid to evaporate faster.

WATER RISES ON ITS OWN

Explanation

In a puddle, a glass of water, or the ocean, every water molecule is attracted to all of the water molecules surrounding it. This means every water molecule is pulled equally in every direction. But the molecules at the very top are pulled in every direction but up, because they are the surface of the liquid. These molecules form something like a "skin" at the water's surface. This "skin" is an example of surface tension. Surface tension is what we call the ability of water molecules to stick to each other.

BACKGROUND INFORMATION

Surface tension allows water to be drawn up the stalks of flowers, plants and trees. The narrower the walls of a container or tube are, the greater the distance the water can move upward. Water molecules can be attracted to the surfaces around the liquid, such as the interior wall of a drinking glass, the walls of a thin glass tube or the walls of the tubes that run up a celery stalk. As the molecules are attracted to both the surrounding walls and to each other, they pull each other up the container's inner walls. This process is called *capillary action*. Almost every plant has tiny tubes, called capillaries, through which water rises.

This same capillary action allows us to dry ourselves with a towel after we take a shower. The capillaries in bath towels draw the water into the towel and away from our bodies. Sponges and paper towels absorb water in the same manner.

Experimental Question

How can we prove that water rises up an inner surface on its own?

Necessary Materials

- Two transparent covers of plastic, CD jewel cases
- A piece of thin cardboard cut from a cereal box 3″ by ½″
- Cellophane tape
- A flat pan at least 6″ x 6″ or with at least a 6″ diameter
- Modeling clay

Preparation

None necessary.

Procedure

1. Place the jewel case covers together so that the flat sides are against each other.
2. Fasten one side of the covers together with the cellophane tape.
3. Place the cardboard strip inside the covers at the opposite side.
4. Secure this side with cellophane tape.
5. Put ¼″ of water at the bottom of the pan
6. Make two balls of clay, approximately 1″ diameter.
7. Stand the jewel cases in the water. The taped sides of the cardboard spacer should be perpendicular (up and down) to the water's surface.
8. Put the balls of clay on either side of the jewel cases so that they don't fall down.
9. Examine and record what happens between the jewel case covers.

Results

The water has risen higher on one side than on the other. (**SEE ILLUSTRATION "A."**)

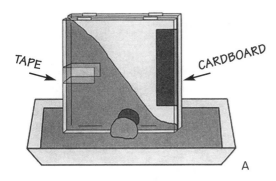

A

But the water level is much lower on the side with the piece of cardboard. Why? Surface tension and the water molecules sticking to the plastic cause the water to climb between the cases via capillary action. Where the cases are closest together, the space through which the water climbs is narrowest. The water climbs the highest at the side of the plastic sandwich where the sides are closest together.

Conclusion

Because of surface tension and capillary action, water rises up a narrow container without any outside help. The narrower the tube, the higher up water inside of it can rise.

SECONDARY EXPERIMENT

Experimental Question

How can we show water rising from a plant's roots to its top via capillary action?

Necessary Materials

• A glass half filled with water
• A stalk of celery with leaves on top
• Red food dye
• A watch or clock
• A ruler

Preparation

1. Cut off one stalk of celery at the bottom.
2. Put a couple of drops of dye in the water (be careful not to get the dye on anything that might stain, such as clothing, a carpet or tablecloth).

Procedure

1. Examine the bottom of the celery stalk. Note that the color is green.
2. Place the stalk bottom end down into the colored water. (**SEE ILLUSTRATION "B."**)

B

3. After fifteen minutes, remove the celery from the glass. Examine the side of the celery stalk toward the bottom. Measure and record the distance that the dye has risen in the capillary tubes of the celery stalk.
4. Place the celery back into the glass of dye.
5. Continue to make and record measurements every fifteen minutes for 4 hours.

Results

The water and dye mixture will rise up the stalk of celery. It rises to a much higher level than that of the liquid in which it is sitting. Capillary action causes the water to rise in the celery stalk.

Conclusions

Surface tension, and the ability of water molecules to stick to a surrounding surface, allow water to rise up the narrow tubes called capillaries that are found inside of plants. We can show the results of capillary action by watching a colored liquid rise in a cut flower, a stalk of celery, or any other plant.

THE WEIGHT OF WATER

Explanation
The pressure at the top of a fluid-filled container is less than the pressure halfway down. And the pressure continues to increase all the way to the bottom of the fluid-filled container. Water pressure, like air pressure, is a function of weight. The lower down in a fluid an object is, the more water there is above it, and therefore the more weight there is pressing down on it. Water pressure, like air pressure, is a force that can be measured. We can show visually that water pressure increases along with the depth of a fluid.

Experimental Question
Is the pressure at the bottom of a fluid-filled carton the same as, greater than, or less than it is at the top?

Necessary Materials
- A pitcher
- A paper or plastic milk carton
- Marker pen
- A carpenter's nail
- A sturdy box—a minimum of 6″ on each side
- A plastic shoebox
- Water
- A ruler
- A plastic tablecloth
- A 6″ length of masking tape

Preparation
1. Using the ruler and marker pen, mark points on one side of the milk carton at: 1″ up from the bottom, 4″ from the bottom and 6″ up from the bottom.
2. Using the nail, punch equal-sized small holes in one side of the container at those marks.
3. Place the masking tape over the holes on the outside of the carton.

Procedure
1. Place the tablecloth on your work surface.
2. Put the sturdy box on the tablecloth.
3. The prepared milk container is placed on top of the box near one edge. (The side with the holes is at the box's edge. **SEE ILLUSTRATION.**)
4. The plastic shoebox is placed on the table at the side of the container where it can catch the water.
5. Without moving the milk container, fill it with water from the pitcher.

BACKGROUND INFORMATION

Water is much heavier than air. A cubic foot of air weighs about one ounce. A cubic foot of seawater weighs about 64 pounds. Water exerts more pressure per pound on an object than air does.

The ocean is the largest fluid-filled container that we know of. Although people have no problems with pressure at the surface, as they dive deeper into the water, the pressure builds rapidly. Very soon the pressure becomes so great that people cannot endure it and live. Deep-sea diving suits are specially made to create pressure inside of the suit that equals the pressure from the water on the outside. In this way, the suit keeps the person from being crushed by the water pressure.

6. When the carton is full, remove the masking tape.

7. You may continue to pour water into the top as it comes out through the holes, to make sure that you can observe how far the streams go.

Results

The water will leave the container through the holes in the side and end up in the plastic shoebox. The stream of water from the lowest hole will shoot out the longest. The stream of water from the middle hole will be shorter, and the stream from the top hole will be the shortest of the three.

Conclusion

Because the length of the streams is greater at the bottom, we can conclude that there is greater water pressure at the bottom of the container.

SECONDARY EXPERIMENT

Try using different factors, such as changing the temperature, time of day or type of fluid and do the experiment again. While your results should turn out the same, you should test them to show that these properties don't have an effect on water pressure.

The height of the carton above the table will, however, allow the streams to be longer because they have a chance to reach their full length before hitting the table top.

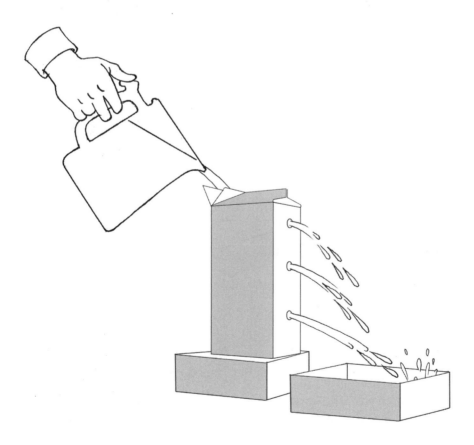

WHY A SUCTION CUP STICKS

Explanation

Did you ever stop to think how a suction cup works? There does not seem to be anything inside to make it stick to your refrigerator door or the tiles in the bathroom. When we push a suction cup down, the volume (amount of space) inside it becomes smaller. By reducing the space inside of the cup, we also push air out of it. This creates an area of lower air pressure inside of the suction cup. (Less air in the same space = less air pressure.) The air pressure outside of the suction cup is so much greater than the pressure inside that the suction cup is pushed against the surface. The lower pressure inside the suction cup allows the greater air pressure from outside to push it against your refrigerator door or any other smooth surface.

Experimental Question

How can we make sure that a suction cup will stick?

Necessary Materials

- 3 suction cups. There should be one of 1″, 2″, and 3″ diameter
- A mirror

BACKGROUND INFORMATION

The reason that a suction cup won't stick to a rough surface is that, while we can push the air out, the little spaces in the rough surface allows some air back in. When we wet the suction cup and press it to a surface, we generally fill up all of the tiny spaces on the surface, which is why it should stick better when wet. The larger the suction cup, the more surface area for the outside air to push against.

- A painted, smooth piece of wood
- An unpainted, smooth piece of wood
- A brick wall
- A ceramic tile—like those used on a bathroom wall
- A fisherman's scale

Preparation

None necessary.

Procedure

1. For this experiment you only have to use the 2″ suction cup. Place it on the various surfaces.
2. Push the suction cup onto the selected surfaces. (**SEE ILLUSTRATION "A."**)
3. Note in your lab book what the surface is and how well the suction cup stuck to it—tight, loose, or not at all.
4. Push the suction cup onto the surface that held it the tightest. Attach the fisherman's scale to the suction cup and measure how much force is needed to pull it off.
5. Next, wet the inside of the suction cup with a few drops of water. Push it against the surface just used. Once again using the scale, measure how much force is needed to pull the wet suction cup from its place.
6. Compare the forces needed to pull the suction cups off when dry and wet. Note how much force is shown just before the suction cup lets go of the surface.

Results

The suction cup will stick better to a smoother surface. The painted wooden surface is flatter and smoother than the unpainted surface. A mirror is the smoothest surface of all. A suction cup usually sticks better when it is wet than when it is dry. (**SEE ILLUSTRATION "B."**)

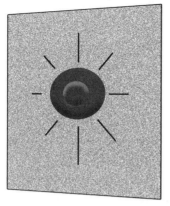

A

Wet   Dry

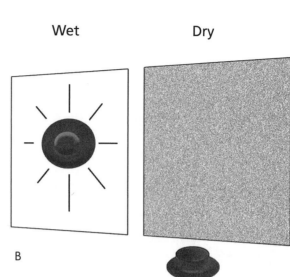

B

Conclusions

The smoother a surface is, the easier it is to make a suction cup stick to that surface. A wet cup will stick better than a dry cup. The more air that can be squeezed out of the cup, the greater the difference between the air pressure on the outside and inside, the better it will stick. The better a suction cup sticks, the more force is required to remove it.

SECONDARY EXPERIMENT

Experimental Question

Will a larger suction cup stick better than a smaller one? Why?

Procedure

1. Repeat the steps from the main experiment using the 2″ suction cup and then the 3″ suction cup.
2. Make sure that you note carefully the amount of force needed to separate the cup from the various surfaces, both when it is dry and when it is wet.

Results

Again, the wet suction cups stick better than the dry ones. The 2″ cup requires more force to remove than the 1″ cup. And the 3″ cup requires more force to remove than the 2″ cup.

Conclusions

A larger suction cup has a larger area for air to press on. More air pressing on the outside makes it harder to remove from a smooth surface. This means that a large suction cup will stick better than a small one.

CREATING A PARACHUTE

Explanation

Air—we can't see it, but we know it's there. Air takes up space and has weight. It takes some kind of force to move through air. People use their muscles to push themselves through the air when they walk. A simple way to confirm the presence of air is to pick a windy day, face into the wind, and run down your street. Then turn around and, with the wind at your back, race back the other way. Running against the wind (which is only moving air) is much harder.

The larger an object is, the larger the area it has to push against the air. The surface of any object will stop the flow of air, causing the air to find a path around the object. This is known as "air resistance." To decrease, or lessen, air resistance, we reduce the amount of surface area that the wind hits. When you are running into the wind, you can do this by bending over a bit and making your body smaller. To increase air resistance, simply create a larger surface area. A parachute is a device that creates a large surface area to resist the wind. This slows an object's fall to earth.

BACKGROUND INFORMATION

Many cars are designed to decrease air resistance. The more air resistance, the more fuel a vehicle needs to travel at a constant speed. Less air resistance means needing to buy less fuel. Sometimes, however, a vehicle that is intended to move fast needs help in stopping. To help it slow down, an airplane raises its flaps to increase air resistance. Drag-racers, which travel over 250 miles per hour, use parachutes to help them slow down. Knowing that a larger surface increases air resistance led to the development of parachutes.

If a person jumped out of a plane without a parachute, he would accelerate until he reached the maximum speed for falling bodies, which is about 120 miles per hour. (It's not a good idea for a human to hit the ground at that speed!) With a parachute, the speed of landing is slowed down to somewhere between 15–30 miles per hour. The parachute slows your fall by increasing the surface area that air molecules hit, which increases air resistance.

Experimental Question

How can we use our knowledge of air resistance to create a better parachute?

Necessary Materials

- 5 identical fishing weights (4 ounce, 5 ounce, or 6 ounce weights)
- Lightweight cotton string
- 4 identical cotton handkerchiefs (should be about 8″ on each side)
- You will need to use an area that has two different levels at least 6 to 8 feet in difference. (A balcony with a railing is perfect. For presentation at your science fair, or if you do not have a balcony, an 8-foot high folding ladder is fine.)

Preparation

Cut the handkerchiefs as follows:

1. Measure off and cut 1″ from all sides of the 1st handkerchief. This will be parachute "B."
2. Measure off and cut 2″ from all sides of the 2nd handkerchief. This will be parachute "C."
3. Cut the third handkerchief in half. Cut this half in half again, so that you are left with a square that is approximately 4″ long on each side. This will be parachute "D."

4. The remaining uncut handkerchief will be called parachute "A."

5. Cut 16 lengths of string, each one 16″ long.

6. Tie four pieces of string—one in each corner—to parachute B.

7. Do the same for the other 3 parachutes.

8. For each parachute, tie all 4 lines to one of the fishing weights. (**SEE ILLUSTRATIONS.**)

Procedure

1. Go to the upper level with all of your equipment including one unattached weight. (If you are using a ladder, place all of your equipment in a box or tray, and carefully carry that up with you to the first rung below the top of the ladder.)

2. Hold the top, center of parachute "A" with your fingertips in one hand, and the weight with the fingertips of the other. Which one do you think will hit the ground first if you release them at the same time? Drop them and see if your guess was correct.

3. Repeat the experiment a number of times using the other parachutes and note your results.

4. Drop the "A" parachute and the "B" parachute at the same time. Note your results. Then drop the "A" parachute with the "C" parachute at the same time. Finally, Drop the "A" parachute with "D" at the same time. Record all of your results.

5. Record on a chart the size of each parachute (or the *area*, for more advanced students) and how long it takes to fall.

Results

The largest parachute falls the slowest. The smallest parachute falls the fastest. The weight, by itself, falls much faster than any of the parachutes.

Conclusion

The larger the parachute, the more it slows the rate at which an object falls.

The parachute with the greatest surface area (parachute "A") is the one that takes the longest time to hit the ground because it offers the most air resistance. More air molecules are hitting it, which slows its rate of descent.

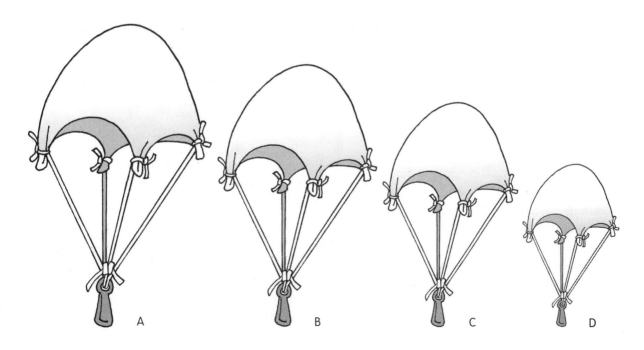

A   B   C   D

HOW TO AFFECT AIR AND WATER PRESSURE

Explanation: You've seen that creating a difference in air pressure from the inside of an object to the outside of the object can have a dramatic effect ("Why a Suction Cup Sticks"). A suction cup will stick to a flat surface once the air inside of it (and hence the air pressure) is less than the air (and air pressure) on the outside. We can use other, simple methods to change the pressure around an object with equally dramatic results. We can make objects move in surprising ways.

Experimental Question: What will happen when a fast moving stream of fluid (air or water) flows between two objects?

Necessary Materials
- Two identical 2″ Styrofoam™ balls
- A needle
- Thread
- Sticky tape

BACKGROUND INFORMATION

The Swiss scientist, Daniel Bernoulli discovered and developed many important theories in both science and mathematics. One theory—the results of which we see every day—is named after him. It is called the Bernoulli Principle. Bernoulli surmised that as a fluid moves faster, the pressure within the fluid decreases. This applies to both gases (air) and liquids (water). Airplanes fly, in large part, due to the fact that air is moving faster over the top of, and slower under the bottom of, their wings. The top of the wing has less force pushing down on top than the bottom has pressure pushing up. This difference in pressure helps the plane to lift.

- Two identical hair dryers
- Two floating toy boats
- A hot water bottle with tubing
- A basin filled with water
- Two pieces of paper 1″ wide by 11″ long
- A ping pong ball
- A funnel
- A circular, oscillating, portable house fan
- A beach ball

Preparation: Part One
1. Using the needle, pass a separate 18″ length of thread through the center of each ball.
2. Secure the thread at the bottom of the ball with a knot and sticky tape.
3. You should have 2 Styrofoam™ balls securely attached to the end of two separate 18″ lengths of thread.
4. Tape the free ends of the threads to the top of a table. The balls should be at the same height and about 1″ apart.

Procedure: Part One
1. Try to push the balls apart by pursing your lips and blowing a stream of air between them. What happens?
2. Perhaps you could not blow hard enough. Use a hair dryer to direct a flow of air between the balls. (**SEE ILLUSTRATION "A."**) What happens?

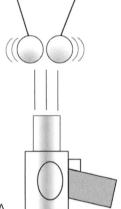

A

Results: Blowing between the two balls makes them move closer to each other, not further away. Blowing a stream of faster moving air between them with the hair dryer actually brings them even closer together.

Conclusion: The fast moving current of air decreases the pressure between the two balls and the surrounding air pressure pushes them together. A slower moving current of air has the same effect but to a lesser degree.

Preparation: None necessary.

Procedure: Part Two

1. You'll need two hair dryers for this one.
2. Take one hair dryer in each hand.
3. Aim the flow of the right hand dryer to the right of the righthand ball.
4. Aim the flow of air from the left one to the left of the lefthand ball (**SEE ILLUSTRATION "B."**) What happens?

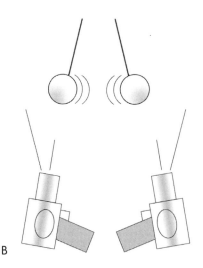

B

Results: The balls should separate because of the lower air pressure created by the streams of air on the far side of each ball.

Conclusions

A fast moving stream of air has less pressure within than the surrounding air. Two streams of fast-moving air on the outer sides of the two balls lessens the pressure on the outside. The pressure between the two balls is now greater than the pressure on the outside of the two balls. This greater pressure will cause the two balls to move apart.

SECONDARY EXPERIMENT

Experimental Question
Will a fast moving stream of water act to lower pressure the same as a fast moving stream of air?

Preparation
1. Fill the water bottle with lukewarm water.
2. Place the rubber tube in the opening of the water bottle.
3. Place the two toy boats in the basin, side by side. They should be near each other but not touching, about 1″ apart.

Procedure
1. Hold the rubber tube near the opening, and place it on the surface of the water.
2. Place the tube so that it is pointing to the space between the two boats.
3. Wait until the water is calm and the boats are not moving.
4. Squeeze the water bottle, so that the stream of water flows between the two boats.
5. Try this a few times, each time moving the boats 1″ further apart.

Results
The faster moving stream of fluid coming from the tube will actually make the two boats move closer together.

Conclusions
A fast moving stream of water will create lower pressure inside than the pressure outside, just as a fast moving stream of air will.

THE CARTESIAN DIVER

Explanation

Submarines make use of pressure and density to dive and surface without using their engines. Submarines have empty chambers called ballast tanks. When the commander of the sub wants the ship to dive, he orders the chambers to be flooded with seawater. When water enters the ballast tanks, the submarine's weight increases, as does its density (more mass in the same amount of space). This makes the sub sink. The captain can also order the ballast tanks to be emptied, which will decrease the weight (and density) of the sub, and the ship will rise. One experiment that shows how pressure and density affect an object's ability to float or sink is called "the Cartesian Diver."

BACKGROUND INFORMATION

It is easy to compress air. (Compression means squeezing the same amount of a substance into a smaller space.) You can take the amount of air that fills an empty juice bottle and compress it to fit a space half the size. Water, on the other hand, does not compress well at all. It is impossible to squeeze the amount of water that fills a juice bottle into a space half that size.

Density is a measure of how much of a substance fits into a particular volume, or space. When we take a substance—like air—and compress it into a smaller space, we are making that substance more dense. We say that we have *increased its density*. Confined to a space half the size of its original container, the air has become twice as dense. Pressure can be used on a variety of substances to make them *more dense*.

Experimental Question

How can we show that density and pressure play a part in a submarine's ability to dive and surface?

Necessary Materials

- An eye dropper
- Some BB's or other small weights
- An 8″ deep cooking pot
- A clean empty plastic soda bottle with its screw-on top
- Water
- A piece of sponge about 2″ square
- A small piece of wood
- A small piece of paper towel
- A marble
- An iron washer that you can find in a hardware store
- A cork
- An aluminum foil pie plate
- An accurate kitchen scale

Preparation

1. Fill the cooking pot with water to within 1″ of the rim.

Procedure: Part One

1. Place the sponge, piece of wood, marble, pie plate, washer and cork in the cooking pot, one at a time. Record which ones sink and which ones float.
2. The sponge, cork, wood and pie plate should float. The washer and marble should sink.
3. Weigh each item and record the weight.
4. Crumple the pie plate into a tight ball. Reweigh the pie plate. Does it weigh the same as before it was crumpled?
5. Place it in the cooking pot. What happens?

Results

The crumpled pie plate should sink.

Conclusions

When an object is less dense than water, it floats. When an object is denser than water, it sinks. Density (how much matter is packed into a particular space) is determined by two things; the volume (size–height width, depth) of an object, and its weight. If it is relatively large, but lightweight, like a cork or piece of sponge, it is less dense than water and will float. If it is relatively small and heavy, it is more dense than water and will sink. The reason that the pie pan floated is that its volume was relatively large compared to its weight. When you crumpled it up, the volume decreased but the weight stayed the same. This crumpling made it more dense than water, so it sank.

Procedure: Part Two

1. Remove the bulb from the eye dropper.
2. Place a few BB's inside the dropper's tube and replace the bulb.
3. Put the dropper, bulb side up, into the plastic soda bottle, filled with water.
4. The dropper should just be heavy enough to sink slowly. Adjust the number of BB's until the dropper is just barely floating. (**SEE ILLUSTRATION "A."**)
5. Screw the cap tightly onto the bottle.
6. Observe the dropper and how high the water rises inside the dropper's tube.
7. Squeeze the sides of the bottle tightly. What happens to the height of the water inside the dropper's tube? Does it rise, fall or remain the same? Record your observations.

   What happens to the dropper when you squeeze the bottle

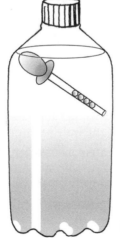

A

harder? Does it stay in place or sink to the bottom of the bottle? Record your observations. (**SEE ILLUSTRATION "B."**)
8. Stop squeezing the bottle. What happens to the water in the dropper's tube? What happens to the dropper? Record your observations.

Results

When the bottle is squeezed, more water enters through the bottom of the eye dropper. The dropper begins to sink. When the squeezing stops, some water leaves the eye dropper, and it begins to rise once again.

Conclusions

When the bottle is squeezed, the pressure in the bottle is increased. It is difficult to compress water but easy to compress (squeeze together) air. Because you have increased pressure in the bottle, the water has no where to go but into the dropper's tube. The air in the dropper gets compressed as water enters the tube. When water enters the tube it increases the tube's weight and density. If we decrease the pressure on the bottle, and therefore on the eye dropper, we also decrease the density (and weight) of the material inside of the dropper, and therefore it will tend to float once again.

B

The experiment called "the Cartesian Diver" is a good example of how pressure and density affect an object's ability to float or sink. Using the forces of pressure and density, a submarine can rise or dive without using its engines.

Explanation

Some things are naturally more dense, other things less dense. To measure the density of objects, we need a starting point. That starting point is fresh water. Pure water has a density of 1 and every other item's density is compared to the density of pure water. Ice, frozen water, has a density lower than 1, which is why it floats. Salt water, like the water in the oceans, has a density greater than 1.

Experimental Question

Can we determine if water is fresh or salty without tasting it?

Materials

- 2 16-ounce measuring cups
- Salt
- One raw, fresh egg (unpeeled)
- Distilled water from a pharmacy or auto supply store (This is to ensure that the water is pure)
- A teaspoon

Preparation

1. Fill both cups half way with distilled water.
2. Place two spoonfuls of salt into one of the cups and stir until all of the salt has dissolved.
3. Keep on adding and stirring in salt, one spoonful at a time, until no more salt dissolves.
4. The water will probably stay cloudy because there will be undissolved particles suspended in it, giving the water a less than clear appearance. Prepare the salt water a day or so in advance. You should end up with crystal clear water as the undissolved salt settles to the bottom of the cup.

DISTILLED WATER

C

SALTY WATER

D

Procedure

1. Gently place the egg in the plain water. Does it float or sink? (**SEE ILLUSTRATION "C."**)
2. Remove the egg and gently place it in the salt water. What happens to the egg? Does it float or sink? Record your observations. (**SEE ILLUSTRATION "D."**)

Results

The egg will sink in the distilled water, and float in the salty water.

Conclusion

It is possible to discover if water is salty or fresh by testing its density. Salt water is denser than fresh water, and can float an egg, but fresh water cannot. (If you were to measure exactly 1 ounce of each on a sensitive scale, one would find that the salt water weighs more than the fresh water. This is because salt water is denser.)

HOW A JET ENGINE WORKS

Explanation

Did you ever wonder how jet planes fly? When we see planes live or in pictures, we sometimes see a stream of fire coming from the engines' exhaust tubes. Sometimes we see a cloudy trail following a jet as it flies across the sky. This happens because a jet engine takes in air as it moves forward. The air is heated, compressed, and sent through the blades of the engine. The air then mixes with jet fuel. This mixture is ignited. The combustion (burning) of the mixture turns the engine's turbine blades very rapidly, which causes even more air to be sucked through the blades. The smoke produced by the combustion is forced out through the

BACKGROUND INFORMATION

Newton's Third Law of Motion states: "For every action, there is an equal and opposite reaction." A simple example of this can be seen by putting on a pair of roller skates (traditional four-wheel or in-line; makes no difference). Hold a basketball in your hand while standing still. Then throw the ball hard in front of you. The force of your action—throwing the ball—will cause an equal and opposite reaction: you will move backward on your skates. The harder you throw the ball, the further backward you will move because the force of reaction is equal to the force of the initial action. In the case of a plane, the "action" is the exhaust from the burning of the air-and-fuel mixture being forced out the backs of the engines. The "reaction" is the plane moving forward. A turbine engine is a perfect example of a machine that uses Newton's Third Law.

exhaust tubes in the rear of each engine. The exhaust also contains water vapor. The thin white lines we see following a jet plane (called "contrails") are caused by the water vapor condensing. This appears in the sky as a trail of white streaky clouds. The force of the exhaust moving backward pushes the plane forward.

Experimental Question

How do objects react when acted upon by a force?

Necessary Materials

- A plastic soda or water bottle
- Plastic soft drink straws
- String
- Water
- A funnel
- Silicone sealing glue
- Two folding chairs
- A broomstick
- A large catch basin at least 2 feet in diameter
- Masking tape
- A small amount of modeling clay

Preparation

Have an adult help you with all of the preparation.

1. Pierce 2 holes in the plastic bottle's side. The holes should be a little smaller than the diameter of the straws.
2. The holes should be near the bottom and directly opposite each other.
3. Cut two 3″ sections from the straw.
4. Insert one section in each hole.
5. Spread the glue around the straw, where the straw enters the bottle. You want to secure the straw in place and prevent water from leaking out of the hole. The

straws should be aimed in opposite directions to each other.

6. When the glue is dry, put a small ball of clay into the opening of each of the straws. This will prevent water from escaping while you fill the bottle.

7. Make a loop in the center of each of the two pieces of string.

8. Place both loops around the neck of the bottle and tie each in place, with one loop on either side of the neck.

9. The two ends of the strings should be opposite each other on the bottle's neck (or as opposite as possible).

10. The bottle should be hanging from the ends of the strings and centered (that is, not leaning to one side). If the bottle is NOT centered, adjust the positions of the loops until it is.

11. Place two folding chairs back to back, about 2 feet apart.

12. Lay a broom handle across the backs of both chairs.

13. Secure the broomstick in place with a few long pieces of masking tape.

14. Tie the free ends of the strings to the center of the broomstick.

15. The bottom of the bottle should be 6″ to 10″ away from the back of each chair.

Procedure

1. Place the funnel in the mouth of the bottle.

2. Hold the funnel and bottle together, keeping them from moving, and fill the bottle with water. (**SEE ILLUSTRATION "A."**)

3. Once the bottle is filled, remove the funnel and release the bottle.

4. Remove the small pieces of clay that are in the ends of the two straws.

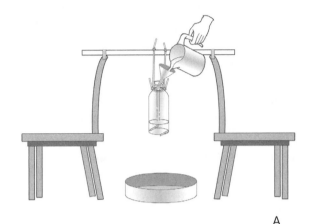

A

5. What happens? Why do think that happens?

Results

As water begins to stream out from the holes at the bottom of the bottle, the bottle begins to spin. (**SEE ILLUSTRATION "B."**)

Conclusions

The action observed is the water moving away with force through the bottle's two oppositely placed straws. The reaction of the bottle to this force is to spin.

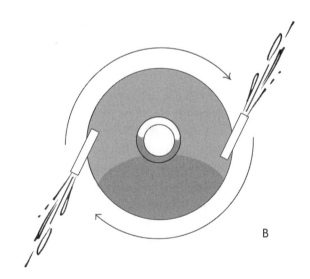

B

SECONDARY EXPERIMENT

Experimental Question: How will a balloon react when air is let out of its valve?

Necessary Materials

- Long rubber balloons—these work better than the round kind
- A soda straw
- A scissors
- 12 feet of string
- Sticky tape
- Two chairs

Preparation

1. Place the two chairs back to back 6 feet apart.
2. Tie the string to the back of one chair.
3. Cut the straw into 5″ lengths.
4. Inflate one balloon and twist but do not tie the end.
5. Tape one piece of straw to the balloon. The length of the straw should be in the direction of the balloon's length.
6. Place the free end of the string through the straw.
7. Tie the free end of the string to the second chair's back.
8. Move the chairs apart so the string has little to no sag.
9. Move the balloon and straw on the string so that the valve end is almost touching one chair. (**SEE ILLUSTRATION "C."**)
10. Insert the second length of straw into the valve end of the balloon. (Keep your finger over the open end of the straw to keep the air from coming out.)

Procedure

1. Remove your finger from the open end of the straw, allowing the air to escape. What happens?
2. Re-inflate the balloon and repeat the experiment. What happens?

Conclusions: The air leaves the balloon in the direction of the valve. There is a force in that direction. An equal but opposite force is placed upon the balloon, which moves it in the other direction (forward), guided by the string and straw.

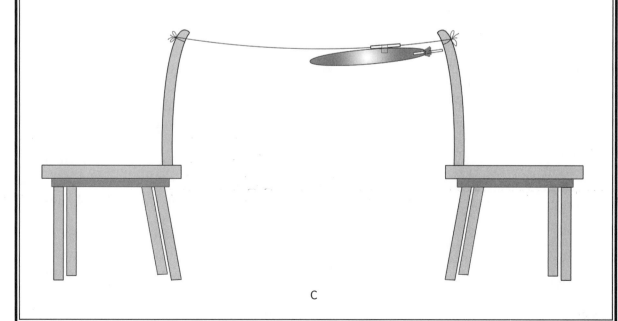

C

PENDULUMS

Explanation

Playground swings are fun. They are so much fun that it's hard to believe they are based upon science. They are examples of pendulums. A pendulum is a string, wire, rope, chain, or bar attached to a support at its upper end with a weight at the lower end. The attachment at the upper end allows the pendulum to swing free. You can go to a playground and honestly tell your folks that you are doing scientific investigations for this experiment. Conduct the experiment on a wind free day.

Experimental Question

Can we tell time with a playground swing?

Necessary Materials

- A stopwatch
- A playground swing

For a tabletop demonstration, you can repeat the experiment with a weighted string tied to a steady overhead support (**SEE ILLUSTRATIONS "A" AND "B."**)

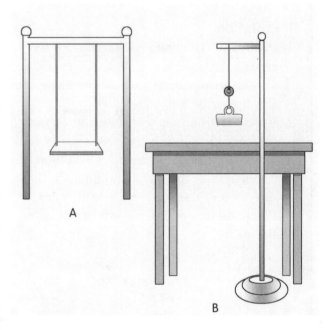
A

B

BACKGROUND INFORMATION

Pisa, Italy where they have the famous "leaning tower," was the home of an important scientist named Galileo Galilei. One day, in 1583, Galileo noticed that a chandelier (which hung down from a ceiling and used candles rather than light bulbs) was swinging back and forth in a steady rhythm. He decided to time how long it took to swing through one round trip. Not having a watch he used his pulse as a timer. He made an amazing discovery. No matter how far the chandelier swung in distance, it always took the same time to make a full trip back and forth. The back-and-forth trip of a pendulum is called the "frequency." As the pendulum swings back and forth, the height that it attains with each swing becomes smaller. (The highest point of each swing is called the "amplitude.") Galileo discovered that even while the amplitude becomes smaller, the pendulum's frequency remains the same. Even with a smaller arc, each swing takes the same amount of time.

Procedure: Part One

1. Have a friend stand behind the swing and pull it back as far as he or she can.
2. Keeping the chain or rope as straight as possible helps to keep the chain and swing from whipping about. Your helper is to let the swing go on your command.
3. Using the stop watch, measure from the time they let it go, to the time it comes back to its starting point. Record that time.
4. Allow the swing to continue its pendulum action without stopping it.

5. Time every 5th round trip of the swing. Note the time of that swing.
6. Have your friend note the approximate height the swing reaches every 5th time that it comes back to him.
7. What do you notice about the HEIGHT (amplitude) of the swing as the experiment goes on? Is the distance the same each time? Is it different?
8. What do you notice about the TIME (frequency) for a complete back and forth trip?

Results

The swing moves in shorter and shorter arcs as time goes by. Even though the arcs grow shorter, the time that it takes to complete one back and forth trip remains the same.

Conclusions

The length of time of each round trip is a measure of the pendulum's "frequency." The frequency will remain the same, even as the amplitude of each swing gets smaller.

Procedure: Part Two

1. Using your stopwatch, you now know how to determine the swing's frequency.
2. Now that you know how many seconds it takes for the swing to make a round trip (the swing's frequency), you can use the swing as a timer.
3. If the swing's frequency is 6 seconds, you know that 5 complete round trips is 30 seconds, or a half a minute. (Multiply the frequency by the number of round trips.)

SECONDARY EXPERIMENT

Experimental Question

Does the amount of weight at the bottom end of the pendulum have anything to do with its frequency?

Necessary Materials

- String
- A bulldog clip (stationary store)
- A marker pen
- A number of heavy metal washers
- A sturdy overhead support to hold the pendulum
- A stop watch

Procedure

1. Tie the string to the support.
2. Place a washer on the free end of the string.
3. Attach the bulldog clip to the end of the string to keep the washer from falling off.
4. Mark the exact spot on the string where the jaws of the clip are.
5. Time and record the frequency of the pendulum through 3 round trips.
6. Stop the pendulum. Remove the clip and add one washer to the string.
7. Replace the clip to the same spot.
8. Time and record the frequency of the pendulum through 3 round trips.
9. Stop the pendulum. Remove the clip and add 5 more washers to the string. Replace the clip to the same spot.
10. Time and record the frequency of the pendulum through 3 round trips.
11. Compare the times. What are the results?

Results

The frequency of your pendulum should be the same no matter how much weight is at the end of the pendulum.

Conclusion

Apparently, weight is not a factor in the frequency of a pendulum.

USING AN INCLINED PLANE

Explanation

The force needed to lift an object is equal to the object's weight. A five-pound brick takes five pounds of force to lift by hand. When the same object is raised by being pulled up an inclined plane, less force is needed from the person lifting it. Less force is needed because the simple machine helps do the work.

Experimental Question

How can a simple machine make it easier to lift heavy objects?

BACKGROUND INFORMATION

A machine is a device that makes work easier. Machines do this by decreasing the force (a push or a pull) necessary to do a job.

There are five types of simple machines. They are: **The inclined plane** (which we know best as a ramp), generally used to raise or lower heavy objects by rolling or sliding. **The screw**, which is a type of inclined plane that is wrapped around itself. **The pulley**, which is a wheel with a grooved rim in which a pulled rope or chain moves to change the direction of the pull. **The wheel and axle**. The axle is a bar that runs through the center of the wheel. When the wheel is turned, the axle moves. The fifth type of simple machine is **the lever**. It is used to increase, transmit and sometimes change the direction of a force. This is usually a sticklike object that works to increase either the force applied to an object or the distance an object is moved.

Necessary Materials

- A solid wooden plank (preferably pine) 1″ thick x 6″ wide x 36″ long
- Two bricks
- A toy truck large enough to securely hold a brick
- A fisherman's scale that measures in ounces

Preparation

1. Place one brick flat on a surface. (If doing this on your kitchen table, place some newspaper on the table first so that you won't scratch the surface.)
2. Place one end of the plank atop the second brick, and its other end on the tabletop (or whatever surface you're using) to create an inclined plane.

Procedure

1. Weigh the brick and the truck with the scale.
2. Add the weights together and record the total.
3. Place the brick on the truck. (**SEE ILLUSTRATION "A."**)
4. Attach one end of the scale to the front of the truck.
5. Start to pull the truck up the ramp using the scale. (**SEE ILLUSTRATION "B."**)
6. As you are pulling, read the amount indicated on the scale.

Results

The force needed to pull the truck up the inclined plane is less than the weight of the brick and truck. The inclined plane makes it easier to raise the truck and brick off the ground.

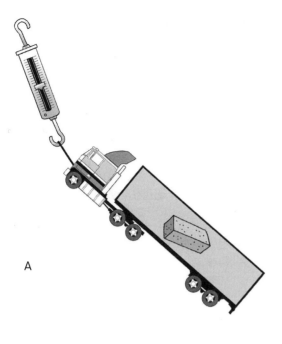

A

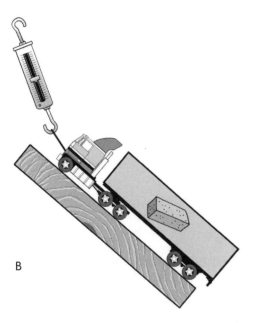

B

SECONDARY EXPERIMENT

This is a "thought experiment." You don't have to actually do it, just picture it in your mind. Then you can make a chart to show how this would be done.

1. Imagine that you have a 50-pound bag of concrete that you must move from the ground to the trunk of a car. The opening of the trunk is 2 feet above ground level.
2. If you put the bag on the ground at the back of the car and pick it up, you will have to exert 50 pounds of force.
3. You can do less work to accomplish the same task by using an inclined plane. Imagine that you place a plank of wood, 1 foot wide by 8 feet long, from the back of the car to the ground.
4. Then you tie up the 50-pound bag and pull it up the plane to the trunk.
5. This is much easier than picking the bag straight up from the ground. In fact, the amount of force it takes to pull the bag up the plank would only be 12½ pounds.

Conclusions
Simple machines make work easier. An inclined plane is one such machine.

Conclusions

An inclined plane reduces the force a person must use to pull or lift heavy objects from one level to another. If you have an inclined plane (ramp) 3 feet long, and want to lift an object 1 foot in the air, the force needed to pull or push it up the ramp is only ⅓ what would be needed to lift up the object by hand.

MAKING AND READING COMPASSES

Explanation

Finding your way around the world is made much easier by knowing in which direction you are moving. A compass is a simple device that always points in the same direction: magnetic north. If you are traveling by boat or airplane, walking in the forest or just walking around a new city, a compass can keep you from getting lost.

Experimental Question

How can we use Earth's magnetic field to find directions?

Necessary Materials

- A bar magnet
- Iron filings
- Top of a cardboard shoe box
- A clear plastic cup or glass
- A cork

BACKGROUND INFORMATION

Earth is like a giant magnet. It has a North magnetic pole and a South magnetic pole. All magnets that we commonly use also have a north pole and a south pole. A compass is a device that uses a magnetized piece of steel to point to magnetic north. Once you know where north is, you can always find the other three cardinal directions: south, east and west. Turn so that you are facing north. Directly behind you is "south." Raise your right arm straight out and point your index finger: that is "east." Raise your left arm straight out and point your index finger: that is "west." The word "news" is made up of the first letters from the four directions, because "news" means events from all corners of the world.

- A sewing needle
- A knife or razor blade
- A Sharpie or other marker

Preparation

1. Cut the top half-inch of the cork off horizontally.

Part One: Finding a Magnet's Poles

Procedure

1. Sprinkle a bunch of iron filings into the top of a shoe box.
2. Take the bar magnet and place it on a table.
3. Take the shoebox with the filings and hold it on top of the bar magnet. Gently tap the bottom of the box.
4. Watch how the filings line up and record what you see.

Results

The iron filings will spread out in curves from one end of the magnet to its other end. These are called "lines of force," and they spread from one of the magnet's poles to its other pole.

Conclusions

A magnet's north and south poles are at either end of the magnet.

Part Two: Making Your Own Compass

Procedure

1. Fill your cup almost to the top with water.
2. Place the top of the cork gently on the water, with the flat end up.
3. Take your needle and stroke it 25 times on the bar magnet, always stroking in the same direction.
4. Place the needle gently across the top of the cork.
5. Wait until the needle stops moving. (**SEE**

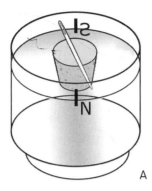

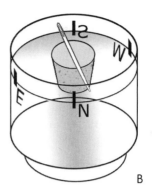

A   B

ILLUSTRATION "A.")

6. Make a dot on the cup/glass where the front of the needle is.

7. Make two dots on the cup/glass where the back end of the needle is.

8. One of these represents magnetic north. The other represents magnetic south.

9. Take your store-bought compass and place it on the table next to your home-made compass.

10. Turn the compass slowly until the needle is pointing to the "N" (for north).

11. Look at the compass you made. Slowly turn the cup/glass so that the single dot points in the same direction as the "N" on the compass you bought. Your needle should still be pointing at the single dot you marked for "North."

12. You now have confirmed that your compass points to the north.

13. On the outside of the cup/glass, mark the letter "N" below the single dot. Mark the letter "S" on the cup/glass below the double dots. Halfway between the "N" and the "S" on the right, mark the letter "E" (for east). Halfway between the "N" and the "S" on the left, mark the letter "W" (for west). (**SEE ILLUSTRATION "B."**)

Results

A magnetized piece of steel can act as a compass if allowed to float.

Conclusions

If we can identify which direction is north, we can figure out where south, east, and west are.

Part Three: Using a Compass to Make a Map

Necessary Materials

- Store-bought compass
- Notebook
- Pen or pencil

Procedure

1. Your map will be from your home to a particular destination. Pick a place that you can walk to in about 15-20 minutes.

2. Walk out of your home and onto the street. Take out your compass.

3. Begin walking toward your destination.

4. Note the direction in which you are walking by checking the compass. Make sure that the compass needle is always pointing "north."

5. Check the compass direction. If you are walking in the same direction as the needle is pointing, you know that you are walking north. But even if you're not walking in the direction that the needle is not pointing, you can still figure out what your direction is. Look at the compass: what letter or letters are in the direction in which you are walking?

6. Note the letter or letters in which you are

walking. (In addition to the four main directions, compasses also show northeast and northwest, southeast and southwest, etc.)

7. When you cross a street or turn a corner, check your compass again.

8. Note in your book how many blocks (or streets) you walk in the same direction. Every time you change direction, note it in your book. Mark down how many streets in the same direction you are walking.

9. Continue to check your compass and note directions as you walk to your destination.

10. When you return home, your notebook should have the directions from your house to your chosen destination, such as: Two blocks north, followed by two blocks east, followed by four blocks north.

11. Turn the notes into a map. Begin it at your home and end it at your destination. Do not include street names, but make sure

you get the number of streets correct in each direction.

12. Get a classmate, family member or neighbor to help you out. Begin outside of your home. Give your helper a compass (make sure he or she knows how to read it.) Ask your helped to follow the directions and walk from your home to the destination you mapped. Could he or she get there just by following your map?

Results

Using a compass can get you from one place to another even if you don't know the names of the streets. Compasses work by pointing to Earth's magnetic north pole.

Conclusions

Compasses can be used to find out what direction you are traveling in as well as the direction you would like to be traveling in.

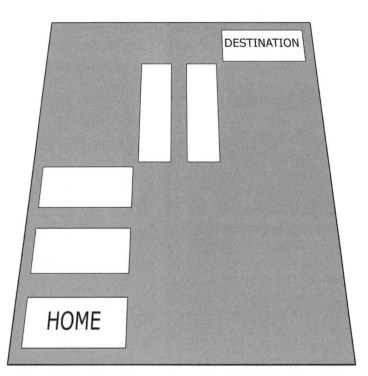

Sample directions: Two blocks north, then two blocks east, then two blocks north.

WHERE ARE THE GERMS?

Explanation

Germs can make us sick. They can give us colds, infections, ear aches, make us throw up, and even give us diarrhea. Germs can be transferred from one person to another, from a pet dog or cat to a person, or even from common objects to a person. Germs are also found in sneezes, in dirty water, and in food gone bad. If we know the places germs are found, we can better prevent ourselves from becoming sick.

Experimental Questions

Where can we find germs? Does washing your hands with soap and water help prevent the spread of germs?

Materials

- A pot in which you can boil water
- Water
- A clean, plastic container with a press-on or screw-on top
- Anti-bacterial soap
- 3 large (baking) potatoes

BACKGROUND INFORMATION

The living creatures we call "germs" are microorganisms (my-kro-OR-gan-izms). This means they are so small they can only be seen through a microscope. There are different kinds of germs, but the ones that cause most of our problems are either bacteria or viruses. Viruses cause colds and flus. Bacteria cause infections and stomach problems, sore throats, fevers and pneumonia. But most bacteria can be killed by anti-bacterial soaps.

- A potato peeler
- A slotted cooking spoon
- Unused, zipper type, plastic sandwich bags
- 5 shoe boxes
- Marker pen

Preparation

1. Wash the plastic container with anti-bacterial soap and water.
2. Have an adult bring the water to a boil and allow it to boil for 5 minutes. This should kill any germs in the water.
3. When the water has boiled for five minutes, allow it to cool down to room temperature.
4. Pour the water into the plastic container.
5. Wash your hands thoroughly with anti-bacterial soap and water.
6. Wash the potatoes with the same soap to get rid of any dirt and kill any germs.
7. Have an adult sterilize the potato peeler, knife, and slotted spoon, by either placing them in boiling water, or washing them with anti-bacterial soap.
8. Peel the potatoes. Do not allow the potatoes to touch the counter or tabletop. Discard the peels.
9. Have an adult cut each potato into 5 approximately equal parts. This will give you a total of 15 pieces.
10. As you cut each potato, place the pieces into the plastic container.
11. When you have finished cutting the potatoes, seal the pieces in the plastic container.
12. Label the shoe boxes "Unwashed Hands," "Extra Dirty Hands," "Rinsed Hands," "Washed Hands," and "Untouched by Human Hands."

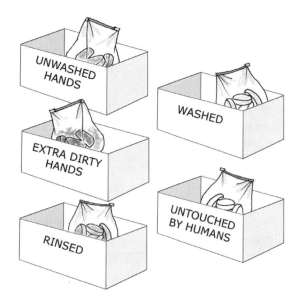

Procedure

1. You will need to recruit 3 volunteers and have each one perform four different tasks for this experiment.
2. Wash your hands with anti-bacterial soap.
3. Open three bags without touching the insides.
4. Using the sterilized spoon, place three of the potato pieces into one bag each.
5. Seal the bags.
6. Use the marker to number the bags, 1, 2, and 3.
7. Put these bags into the "Untouched by Human Hands" box.

Test One

The first test should be done after your three volunteers have been playing normally or doing school work.

1. Using the spoon (do not let the spoon touch their hands), hand them one piece of potato each.
2. Ask them to rub their hands all over the potato.
3. Have each of them open up a plastic bag, put their potato inside, and reseal the bag.
4. Mark each bag with a number or your friend's name.

5. Put these bags into the "Unwashed Hands" box.

Test Two

For the second test, ask your volunteers to rub their hands with dirt from the street or a park.

1. Have them rub a potato piece, place it and seal it in a plastic bag.
2. These bags go in the "Extra Dirty Hands" box.
3. Number each bag.
4. When the volunteers are finished, have them wash their hands with anti-bacterial soap and water.

Test Three

Next, have your volunteers rub their hands with dirt from the street or a park, then rinse their hands under running water.

1. Give them a potato piece each to rub with their hands.
2. Seal each potato into a bag. Number each bag.
3. These go in the box marked "Rinsed Hands."

Test Four

When the subjects are finished, have them wash their hands thoroughly with anti-bacterial soap and water.

1. Give them each a potato piece to rub with their hands.
2. Seal each piece into a bag. Number each bag.
3. Place the bags into the box "Washed Hands" box.

Final Procedure

1. Put all of the boxes in a closet.
2. Examine them every day for four days. Record the look of each bag in each box.
3. Do they have anything growing on them?

If they do, it is probably bacteria.

4. Which has the most? The least?
5. What can you determine about the best way to keep your hands from spreading germs?
6. Record all of your observations and thoughts about how to stop germs from spreading.

Results

The samples in the "Untouched by Human Hands" box should have little to no growth on them. The "Washed Hands" samples should have little to no growth on them. The "Rinsed Hands" sample will have some growth. The "Unwashed Hands" will have more. The "Extra Dirty" samples should have the most growing things.

Conclusion

Unwashed hands pass on many more germs and bacteria than clean hands. This experiment confirms that it is a good idea to wash one's hands frequently, especially before rubbing your eyes, scratching your ears, or holding food in them.

SECONDARY EXPERIMENT

Experimental Question

What common, everyday objects are also likely to pass on germs?

Preparation

1. Prepare some more pieces of raw potato, as in the first experiment.
2. Place them in the plastic container.
3. Take your spoon, some plastic bags and a marker pen, and you are ready for a field trip.

Procedure

1. Rub a piece of potato on an object and seal it in the bag as you did before.
2. Mark each bag with the name of the object the you rubbed the piece of potato on.
3. Here is a list of possible things you want to test for germs:
    - The school's bathroom, door handle or push plate (the inside one) at the end of the school day.
    - A toilet bowl.
    - Hand railings around your neighborhood.
    - A ball that you have been playing with.
    - Paper money and coins. (Should you ever put them in your mouth?)
    - The cafeteria's table tops. (Should you ever place food on them without a plate or piece of paper?)
    - Desk tops.
    - Desk seats.
    - A school book cover.
    - A library book cover.
    - A garbage pail, inside and out.

Results

Each of the above-named objects carries germs.

Conclusions

Germs can be found on many objects we handle every day. The best protection against getting sick from them is to make sure you wash your hands thoroughly before putting them in your mouth or handling food.

RUBBER BANDS DO THE WORK

Explanation: Most of the time when we talk about "energy," we refer to the power of electricity, or even our own feeling of being alert or tired. But in science we also talk about two basic types of energy: energy that is stored, and energy that is in use. Stored energy is called "potential energy," while energy in use is called "kinetic energy." For energy to be used, it must first have been stored. Rubber bands are elastic. That means they can be stretched or pulled out of shape, but when released they return to their original shape. Stretching a rubber band is a way to store energy.

Experimental Question: How can energy be stored and released in a rubber band through the use of a simple machine?

Part One

Necessary Materials
- A box of rubber bands
- A pair of safety goggles

Preparation: None necessary.

Procedure
1. Loop a rubber band around your two index fingers. Touch the rubber band to your lips. Does it feel warm or cool?
2. Stretch the rubber band between your hands and keep it stretched. Touch the rubber band to your lips again. Is it warmer or cooler than when it was unstretched?

Results: When stretched, the rubber band feels warmer.

Conclusion: When we stretch a rubber band, the energy we store in it (potential energy) may be measured by the increase of temperature in the band. The storage and release of energy is always accompanied by a rise in temperature.

Part Two

Necessary Materials
- A large spool without thread
- A rubber band that is slightly longer than the spool is wide
- A toothpick
- A short, unsharpened pencil (golf pencil size is perfect)
- Sticky tape
- Two small metal or plastic washers

Preparation
1. Place the rubber band through the hole in the center of the spool.
2. Place the toothpick through the center of the rubber band on one side of the spool.
3. Break the ends of the toothpick so that it ends up being shorter than the diameter of the spool.

BACKGROUND INFORMATION

When you raise a hammer, you are storing potential energy—the force of gravity that is pulling on it. When you swing the hammer down to drive a nail into a piece of wood, the energy stored in your muscles and the force of gravity is released through the hammer. You have turned potential energy into kinetic energy. Electricity is another type of stored energy. When you press a button or click a switch to turn on a machine (a lamp, or car, or video game, for example), you are releasing the energy into that machine. It can then do the work for which it was intended. You have turned potential energy into kinetic energy.

4. Secure the toothpick in place with the sticky tape.
5. Pull the rubber band out of the other side of the spool.
6. Place the two washers over the rubber band.
7. Put the pencil through the center of the rubber band as in the illustration. (**SEE ILLUSTRATION "A."**)

A

Procedure

1. Wind the pencil in a circle. Have the pencil make at least twenty-five revolutions.
2. Hold the spool and

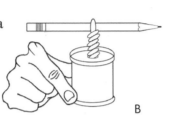

B

pencil firmly in your hand, keeping the pencil from turning.
3. Hold the bottom of the spool to the table top and release the pencil. (**SEE ILLUSTRATION "B."**)

Results: The pencil revolves. The movement of the pencil even causes the spool to move and shake. The potential energy stored in the rubber band was converted to kinetic energy and transferred to the pencil.

Conclusions: Twisting the pencil has stored energy in the rubber band, which gets released when the band untwists. We have created a machine that both stores potential energy and releases it as kinetic energy. Allowing the rubber band to untwist turns the potential energy into kinetic energy, which is transferred to the pencil and spool.

SECONDARY EXPERIMENT

Experimental Question: Why are vice-grip type pliers easier to use than regular (non-locking) pliers?

Necessary Materials

- A standard (non-tension) pair of pliers
- A pair of vice-grip, or locking, pliers
- Two 4″ lengths of heavy-gauge wire
- A wooden dowel

Preparation: None necessary.

Procedure

1. Take a length of wire and bend it around the dowel with your hands.
2. Using the regular pliers, grip both ends of the wire and twist them together until you can no longer twist.
3. Take the second length of wire and bend it around the dowel with your hands.
4. Using the locking pliers, grip both ends of the wire. Then, making sure that the pliers

have locked, twist them together until you can no longer twist.

Results: Could you tell which pliers does the work more easily? Which pliers takes more muscle power to use?

It is easier to twist the wire with a standard pliers than with your hands. But it is much easier to turn it with the locking pliers than with an ordinary pair of pliers.

Conclusion: Using a standard pliers, the energy of your muscles becomes the major force (kinetic energy) in turning the wire, because you must hold the handles together to keep the wire gripped as well as turn it. The locking pliers has a spring and a locking device built into it. When it is applied to the wire, the locking mechanism keeps the pliers' jaws tightly closed. This adds to your muscle power.

FINDING BALANCE POINTS FOR OBJECTS AND YOURSELF

Explanation

An object's center of gravity is the point where gravity pulls downward on every side of an object with equal force. The center of gravity is also referred to as the "balance point" and "center of balance." When carrying an object, whether it is lightweight or heavy, the task is made simpler by finding the object's center of gravity and holding and carrying it at that point.

Experimental Question

How can we find the center of gravity for an object using just our fingers?

Necessary Materials

- A broom
- A 24″ to 36″ dowel (round stick)
- A yardstick or 12″ ruler
- A walking stick (or cane) with a curved handle

Preparation

None necessary.

Procedure: Part One

1. Try to balance the dowel on one finger by placing the stick atop your extended index finger at its middle. If the stick dips down on one side, move it slightly across the top of your balancing finger in the direction of the dipping end. This is called the trial-and-error method.
2. Measure the length of the stick with the ruler. Divide that length in half. Find that halfway point on the dowel. Place your finger under the halfway point. The stick should balance on your finger.
3. Place your hands in front of you. Extend both index (pointer) fingers. The fingers should be level with each other and about

2 feet apart. Have someone place the dowel across your two index fingers. (**SEE ILLUSTRATION "A."**)

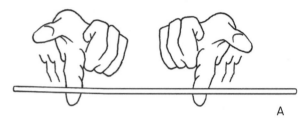

A

4. Close your eyes—you do not need to look at the object to obtain its center of gravity.
5. Keeping the stick level, slowly bring your two index fingers toward each other until they are together.

Results

You will be able to easily find the center of gravity of the dowel so that you can balance it on your two index fingers. Now move the stick slightly to one side, so that it can balance on one finger.

Conclusions

Every lightweight stick-like object has a center of gravity that can be found by allowing our fingers to find its balance point.

BACKGROUND INFORMATION

It is easier to carry any object when it is "balanced" in our hands. This means that the weight on all sides of the object is equal, and it will not tip or fall over as it is carried. When we find that point for any lightweight object, we can actually balance that object by placing a single finger underneath that spot. If the center of gravity is not directly above your finger, the object will not be level and one side will tip lower than the other.

Procedure: Part Two

1. Repeat the same experiments using the broom and a walking stick (cane). You will find the balance point is *not* at the midpoint of either object. (**SEE ILLUSTRATION "B."**)

B

2. This is due to the fact that one end of the broom and one end of the cane has more weight than the other end. The center of balance of such an object is always located closer to the end that has more weight.

3. You should be able to find a balance point for each object by using the technique you used with the dowel. This manner of finding the balance point uses a "built-in" feedback system. You will notice that as you slide your fingers together, one finger will not "want to" move as much as the other one does.

4. If the object begins to tip to one side, you will feel it and automatically move your fingers toward the end that is tipping. This is your "built-in" feedback. Because of this feedback, your fingers will move slowly in fits and starts, until they are next to each other directly under the object's center of gravity.

SECONDARY EXPERIMENT: FINDING YOUR OWN CENTER OF GRAVITY

Experimental Question

How can you find *your* center of gravity in a fast and simple way?

Explanation

You now have proven that the center of gravity, or balance point, for any object is that place where its weight is evenly distributed on all sides. But where is YOUR center of gravity? You can find out by doing the following simple experiment.

Preparation

None necessary.

Procedure

1. Stand with both feet together and slowly lift your left leg, bending it at the knee.
2. Find the position that is most well balanced. Are you standing straight up, or leaning slightly to one side?
3. Stand against a wall with your right arm and shoulder flush against the wall and both feet firmly on the ground next to each other.
4. Now lift your left leg, bending it at the knee. Can you maintain your balance?

Results

While balanced on one leg, your body will lean slightly to one side to find its balance point. When leaning against the wall, it is impossible to lift your outside leg and maintain balance because you cannot shift your body.

Conclusions

A person's center of gravity or balance is in the center of the body, and not over either leg. When one leg is lifted, a person is unbalanced. If the body cannot move to adjust for the unbalanced position, it will not be able to remain upright. In other words, you will fall.

WHAT ANTS EAT . . . AND WHY

Explanation
They're underneath your feet and you hardly ever notice them. But at a picnic or in the park, you usually can't avoid seeing the ants. Even at home, if there's an open window in your kitchen, you might want to check the sugar bowl before using it. Most often you can see ants on the street, usually carrying bits of food much larger than themselves, marching in a straight line back to their anthills. It may seem that anytime you leave some food unattended, you will find ants in it when you return. How, then, can we predict what foods ants actually prefer?

Experimental Question
How can we determine what kind of food ants prefer?

Necessary Materials
• A few ant colonies, preferably within walking distance from your home.
• Just keep on looking at the ground until you find some ants, then follow them back to their little (hopefully) ant hills.
• Once you have found your experimental subjects, you have to decide what to offer them, to see what they like.
• Here is a suggested list (but you can try anything else that comes into your mind).
    Bread—white, whole wheat
    Crackers
    Cookies
    Salt
    Sugar
    Butter
    Cooking oil
    Motor oil
    Vegetable—lettuce, carrots, onions, tomato, cucumber
    Ice cream—different flavors and different brands

    Dishwashing detergent
    Little pieces of hamburger or hot dog
    Sweet relish
    Sauerkraut
    Chips
    Pretzels

It is recommended that you do the experiment with six different types of foods such as a vegetable or fruit, butter, bread, ice cream, sugar and salt.

Procedure
1. Once you have found 2 or 3 different ant colonies, you are ready to proceed. First, you should try to make sure that they are

BACKGROUND INFORMATION

While at first glance ants appear to take any food they can carry, they actually have a preferred diet. A vital element in ants' bodies is a substance called formic acid. All ants manufacture this liquid. Fire ants use it to sting and kill their prey or enemies. Other ants use it to spray over their eggs to protect them from predators. Formic acid can be poisonous. Some birds will place ants in their nests to protect their eggs from parasites such as mites, because the ants will cover the nest with formic acid. Formic acid is composed of the elements carbon, hydrogen, and oxygen. Sugar and carbohydrates—starchy foods like potatoes and corn—are also made from these elements. Finally, sugar and carbohydrates are often called "energy foods" because the body uses their elements to provide quick energy. It makes sense, then, that ants would prefer foods that contain sugars and starches to anything else.

the same kind (species) of ants. There are over 11,000 ant species in the world, but in your town there should be considerably fewer. Make sure they are roughly the same size, the same color, and look alike when viewed through a magnifying glass.

2. The first day you should tempt each colony with the same item. Leave small bits of selected foods three to five feet away from the anthills.

3. Note how they react. Do they seem to like it? Is there a trail of ants leading from the food to the nest? Or are there just a couple of ants tasting the food and then ignoring it?

4. Record your observations.

5. Fill in your chart with these codes:
   A = Like it a lot
   B = Like it somewhat
   C = Do not like it—won't eat it

6. Visit the colonies over the next few days, using a different food each day.

7. Record your results.

8. After you have tested each one of the foods, go back with the three favorite foods.

9. Place each bit of food the same distance away from the colony. Do the ants prefer one food to another?

10. After you have found their favorite, do one more experiment. Go back to the colonies and place the most favorite food 15 feet away, while the not-so-favorite foods are placed 2 feet away from the nest. What are results? Do the ants prefer to go a longer distance to get their favorite foods, or will they take the food they do not like as much, but is easier to reach and take back to the colony?

11. Be sure to record all of your observations.

Results

Ants will almost always prefer sugary foods —and starchy, sugary foods such as potato chips—more than any other types of food.

Conclusion

Sugars and starches are vital to ants in order to help them survive.

	How much do they like salt?	How much do they like sugar?	How much do they like ice cream?	How much do they like butter?	How much do they like vegetables?	How much do they like bread?
Colony #						
1						
2						
3						
4						

OPTICAL ILLUSIONS FOOL THE EYE

Explanation: The five human senses are sight, hearing, smell, touch, and taste. Perception may be described as understanding the information gathered by the senses based upon past experience. Sometimes perception can be fooled. Although we depend on it more than the other senses, it is easy to fool the eye into "seeing" what is not actually there.

Experimental Question

Can we trick people's visual perception?

Materials

• A ruler
• A copy of the accompanying illustration

Preparation: Reproduce and enlarge the following illustration on a photocopy machine. (**SEE ILLUSTRATION "A."**)

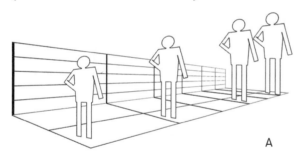

A

Procedure: (You are going to test the visual perception of a number of friends. Before you ask your experimental group the following questions, answer them yourself and record your answers.)

1. Select a group of 5–10 people of varying ages, some youngsters, some teenagers, and some adults.
2. You will be asking them the following questions and recording their answers about the illustration. Each person you question is not to know the answers given by other subjects. Ask the following of each:
3. Which one of these figures of a magician is the tallest?

4. Which one of these figures of a magician is the shortest?
5. Why do you think so?
6. Hand each volunteer the ruler and say, "Please measure the size of each figure. Now that you have measured them, which one is the tallest and which is the shortest?"
7. If anyone says that the magicians are all the same size, ask that person why he/she thinks so. Record that response as well as all of the others.
8. Make a chart separating the subjects by age. Mark their answers in appropriate columns.

Results: Virtually all the people who have never seen this "optical illusion" will say that the tallest is the one on the top and the shortest is the one on the bottom. When they measure the figures, they will see that the magician's are all the same height.

BACKGROUND INFORMATION

Two important aspects of vision are called "depth perception" and "binocular vision." Depth perception is our ability to determine how near or far away an object is. We are very good when objects are fairly close to us—say, ten to twenty feet away—in determining their exact distance. When objects are further away than that, we make guesses based upon past experience. Binocular vision means that the fields of view of our left eye and right eye overlap. The brain places one image atop the other to give us a full view, in three dimensions, of whatever we are looking at. Without a three-dimensional view, we cannot determine how far away an object truly is.

Conclusions: Many people are tricked by the background on which the magicians stand. The background of lines generally makes one think of a long hallway or the side of a building on a street. We have all noticed from everyday life that closer objects look larger than similar objects that are further away—even though we know they are the same size. Based on experience, we "see" the top magician as being further away. But the figure is NOT much smaller than the bottom one, which we register as being "closer" to us. Based on everyday experience, your brain interprets this as follows: "The top figure is further away. But it is not significantly smaller than the bottom one. Therefore, if they were both at the same distance from us, the top one would actually be larger than the bottom one."

SECONDARY EXPERIMENT 1

Experimental Question: Can we create optical illusions with solid, 3-dimensional objects?

Materials
- A piece of light colored construction paper
- A ruler
- A dark marker pen
- Two identical 4″ pieces of soda straw

Preparation
1. Draw a large "V" on the light paper with the marker as in the illustration. (**SEE ILLUSTRATION "B."**)
2. Place one piece of straw near the top center of the "V" so that it crosses both legs. The other piece should lie between the two legs, centered near the bottom so that there is white space between the legs and each end.

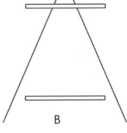

Procedure
1. Ask your test subject, "Which of the lengths of straw looks longer?"
2. Have your subject close his or her eyes or turn around.
3. Switch the positions of the straws, the bottom becoming the top and the top becoming the bottom.

   Ask the question again, "Which one looks longer?"

   Have the subjects pick up both straws and compare them. Are they surprised that they are the same size? If not, ask them why.

Results: Anyone who has never seen this optical illusion before will think that the length of straw that crosses the lines of the "V" is longer than the length that fits within the "V."

Conclusion: The "V" that the straws are resting upon gives clues to the size of each object, just as in the four-magicians puzzle. In the real world, when we look down a street and see lines converging—getting closer together—this is an indication that they are at a great distance from us. Our brain tells us that since the top straw appears to be further away from us, if both were at the same distance the one that started out further away would be larger.

SECONDARY EXPERIMENT 2

Experimental Question
Is it possible to mistake the distance of an object not far from your eye?

Materials
• A yardstick

Preparation
None required.

Procedure
(Carry out the experiment against a blank wall. This will prevent unintentional visual clues to the subjects.)

1. You should use 5 to 10 volunteers for this experiment. No one should see the experiment done before he or she tries it.
2. Have the volunteer hold the yardstick straight out with the right hand. Help the volunteer to point the yardstick at a slight angle, pointing away from him or her.
3. Have the subject close his/her right eye. Have him/her extend the left hand in the same direction as the yardstick. Do not allow a shadow from the hand to be cast upon the yardstick. (**SEE ILLUSTRATION "C."**)
4. Ask him/her to extend the right index finger so it is about 3″ away from the yardstick, just opposite the 13″ mark. Now have him/her bring that finger to the ruler.

Is the finger on the 13″ mark? Or is it in front of or behind the yardstick?

5. Record the results.
6. Repeat the experiment with each of your volunteers, recording the results for each one.

Results
Because they are using only one eye many people will not be able to touch the yardstick when they swing their finger over to it. They will either be in front of or behind it.

Conclusion
It is much easier to estimate relatively close distances when we keep both eyes open. That is why our eyes are separated from each other. Binocular visions gives us depth perception, which enables us to accurately judge distances from us that are not too great.

C